Great Pond

Great Pond

Poems by

Ed Meek

Cover design by Shay Culligan
Cover image from *The Open Book of Nature*
(Adam and Charles Black, 1911)
by Charles Albert, 1872–1965, courtesy of the
Biodiversity Heritage Library New Zealand on Unsplash
Author photo by Ed Meek
Fish illustration by Viktoriya Lissachenko on Unsplash

ISBN: 979-8-90146-903-3

Kelsay Books
502 South 1040 East, A-119
American Fork, Utah 84003
Kelsaybooks.com

Acknowledgments

Thank you to the following publications, in which versions of these poems previously appeared:

Across the Margins: "The Stranger," "Missing the Bus," "Sympathy for the Vandals"
Artemis Journal: "Cats"
The Baltimore Review: "Climate Change"
Berkshire Magazine: "Freedom and the Dignity It Contains"
Blue Mountain Review: "Spirochete"
California Quarterly: "Starry Dynamo"
Cape Cod Times: "Pollen Season," "In Memory Of"
Chicken Soup for the Soul: "Sonnet for the Dead"
Choeofpleirn Press: Rushing Thru the Dark: "Because We Were Happy"
Chronogram: "Installation Art," "Class of 69"
Clerestory: "Mr. Cop," "Great Pond"
Constellations: "Boom Box," "Pedestrian," "Quabbin Reservoir," "Mistaken Identity"
Dash: "Pond Scum," "Grief," "The Death of a Child"
Ekphrastic Review: "Salome"
Goldman Review: "Asylum"
Hole in the Head Review: "Bambino Caravan," "Crown Royal"
Ibbetson Magazine: "In the Provinces"
Light: "Rooms for Rent"
Lowell Review: "Anthropocene."
Meat for Tea: The Valley Review: "In the Dark Room"
Muddy River Poetry Review: "The Great Molasses Disaster"
Nixes Mate: "Wind"
North of Oxford: "Skipping Stones," "Frida Kahlo," "On the Highway"
Poetry Superhighway: "This Rough Beast"
The Red Wheelbarrow: "For Your Sins"
San Pedro Poetry Review: "Hungover Sundays"
Synchronized Chaos: "March with Mookie"

Vita Poetica: "In the Forest," "Passing Away"
WCAI Poetry Sunday: "Northern Cardinal"

"Freedom and the Dignity It Contains" was originally published in *Berkshire Magazine,* August 2022, Courtesy Old Mill Road Media. All rights reserved.

Contents

Skipping Stones

Do you remember keeping your eyes open
for flat, oval rocks to pocket
on walks to the pond?
Saving the best for last, you'd lean
to one side and flick your wrist
flinging the stones just off the water.

It isn't easy to defy gravity
and make a stone skip like a tern
and skim weightless
soaring without wings,
touching down like a plane
while you count until it sinks
and heads to rest anonymous
on the murky bottom.

Maybe that's what we're after
as we try to stay afloat,
skimming on the surface,
defying the odds
for the fleeting feeling of flight.

Climate Change

You woke me up to talk again
about the need to move
when our cat, Isis,
proud as a peacock,
presented us
with a purple finch
she must've caught

outside the window
of our cottage on the coast.

She leapt onto the bed
and dropped her gift
between the white silk sheets.
The bird was as stiff
as a homeless drunk in winter.

Isis returned to her perch on the ledge
and purred with the satisfaction
of a job well done,
while the finch, to our delight,
popped up to its feet,
took to the air and flew out the window.

Was it stunned or playing possum? I wondered.
We have to talk, you said
as I rolled back over feigning sleep.

The Northern Cardinal

The northern cardinal perching
In his brilliant scarlet robes,
his dashing black mask and crown,
dines this May evening
with his demure mate.

He feeds her seeds—head tilted
as if to kiss—to reach her beak.
A bonding ritual, the ornithologist
informs us. Yet it's hard not to find

romance in this annual
springtime performance.
Romance is a myth we need
in times like these.

Looking Back

The Australian crawl isn't a crawl at all
but the swiftest way to swim from here to there,
submersing yourself in the water,
turning your head to catch some air
and admire the scenery passing by
as you slice forward toward your goals.
But should you tire and need a break
you might just flip onto your back and relax—
reaching behind to row the water past your body,
stroking with a view of the sky and what
you've left behind, making it easier to breathe,
but creating a sense of uncertainty
about where exactly you're headed,
and what it is that you really believe.

In Memory Of

In Wellfleet, locals honor the dead
with benches facing the water.
Sit here in remembrance of the lost
they say. Take in the bay or the pond.

On the harbor is a half mile walk
with benches end to end.
Most popular among them,
Susan Birenbaum, 1952–2008.
Her name adorns half a dozen plaques.

I'd like to think she was the Scarlett O'Hara
of her day, a list of young men
on her dance card. More likely,
she was the one who held
the clan together like a rope
holds a boat to a cleat on a dock.

Pollen Season

One morning in early June yellow dust
blown sideways in waves of wind
colonize the earth plant by plant,
blanketing cars, yards and ponds with golden fuzz.
It's nature's promiscuous party
announcing the debut of summer.

On rambles, my dog and I inhale the amber haze—
it coats our lungs as we cough and sneeze
our way back home to collapse on the couch
in a drunk, allergic funk.

Five days in, the pollen frosts our roofs and railings
and cakes the shore of beaches and ponds
where a musty, sulfurous cloud
hangs above the water in a mist.

Like an intermission that lasts too long,
pollen season just won't end
until the rain arrives like a mop
and washes it all away.
The only reminder the fog
that settles in my brain.

Spirochete

—Climate change is a tick's best friend

We're covered in white
from head to foot. We've sprayed ourselves
with poison. We tuck our pants
into our socks—ready for a walk
in the woods with our dog.

Later, while our clothes
tumble in the dryer,
I inspect your body
tweezers in hand
hunting black bugs
anchored with legs—
they cling to your skin
like desperate cats, suck your blood
like vampire bats, and carry
the gift of Lyme:
a Pandora's basket
of deplorable diseases
without the aid of hope.

Like the venom of a snake,
this borrelia bacteria
navigates the bloodstream
to take up residence in the body

an invasive species—
syphilis's twisted sister—
in a fleet of miniature submarines
armed with bio-weapons.
The stand-out—

Powassan, spawn
for seizure, trigger for loss
of memory and the ability
to move independently.
Our dog is immunized
but there is no immunity
for you and me.

Great Pond

Swimming alone late one September afternoon
At Great Pond in Wellfleet, I spotted
Two American Quarter horses emerging from the woods.
Two young girls rode them bareback with ropes for reins.
They were lithe and lovely, tanned in their swimsuits.
I thought they were stopping for water, but the girls
Rode their horses right into the pond,
Slipped off their backs and swam beside them,
Ropes in hand, as if it were the most
Natural thing in the world. Then
They slid back on like seals and rode the horses out,
Disappearing into the woods.
I was momentarily jealous—
How privileged they were!
But the beauty of the scene
Buoyed me up as I floated on my back
Staring at the vast expanse of the sky.

Asteroidea

You may have had an inkling a starfish
isn't a fish at all, but a sea-star?
A fallen angel?

Are you happy or sad to know
it doesn't have a heart or a brain,
a thought or a care in the world?

Still, this puzzling echinoderm
hungers like the rest of us
and scours the sea with the eyes
at the end of its arms
for shellfish and coral
to devour with the mouth
at the center of its body.

Those tiny stems
beneath the arms
are legs! They keep it
on the move
like the stars above.

And what do we owe
this beautiful fallen angel?

June

Although I'm following my feet
as we walk the trail to the beach,
the sun splits the trees and lifts me with its light
as surely as wings lift a bird. And since it is June,
birds abound. Robins find worms, jays steal eggs, hummingbirds
hover over the feeder
and gold-finches compete with butterflies
for our attention. At White Crest Beach
waves carry us all the way to shore
where we toss horseshoes through the thick air
hoping they'll clang against a post
before they're swallowed by the sand.
I spin my unreliable curve
and Eddie hits the white whiffle ball
into the surf where our lab
joyfully retrieves it
to the crowd's delighted cries.
By the time we're back at the house,
margaritas in hand, swordfish charring on the grill,
we've almost had too much of life to contain.

Winter nights, images of waves, will break
on the shores of our dreams.

Fall in New England

It's as if the gods had switched the seasons—
fall when life blooms in a myriad of vibrant shades,
a brilliant display, nature's inimitable array
of diversity: the final symphony

a contrapuntal concert of color—
scarlet-tangerine-copper-lemon-chartreuse—
the pinnacle of the year's work,
the zenith of mother nature's arias.

As if she's singing, can you hear me now?
Do you see how beautiful I am?

Under House Arrest

Trees are never depressed in winter
but we are, under
house arrest, suffering
from light deprivation.

Trees never forget they're trees,
even when the wind dies
and the sun disappears.
But sometimes people
forget they're human
when they're alone,
especially at night.

Trees don't lie
except in the fall,
in a florid, flourish
of colorful excess.
But we lie daily
to ourselves and others
just to survive.

And like us, trees awaken
in spring, sprouting buds,
turning green with promise,
at home with a chorus of birds.

Mustangs

I'd pulled off the highway in Montana
to take a piss. There was no one around, so
I was confused when I felt the ground
tremble beneath my boots
and saw a dust cloud rising like smoke
out of the plains. Then I spotted
a brilliant black stallion
leading a pack of feral mustangs—
galloping for the unharnessed pleasure of speed
as if it were a hundred and fifty years ago
when Blackfeet chased them down for fun.
Now those few wild horses who are left alone
seem unaware of what we've done.
Yet I can't help but smile watching them run.

Bambino Caravan

Spring mornings and late afternoons the daycare children
sprung from Davis Square Kinder Care
toddle past my condo in a lively circus caravan
led by their trainers—Black and Latina queens:

surrogate mother-nanny-nurse-teachers,
who push six-seat carriages, pull octo-bench-carts,
and herd a baker's dozen yellow-vested boys and girls
linked by a walking rope like dwarf horses or baby elephants,
transmogrified into a giant caterpillar,
they migrate through our urban hood.
Meanwhile, the queens tour-guide the names of the sights:
perros y gatos, cherry trees and tulips, robins y *ardillas.*
Vamos ninos! they call. Let's go bambinos!

The Stranger

I was the lucky one who found the stranger
curled up like a cat on the couch on our porch.
I fetched my brother, sister, mom and dad
to check him out. My dad took charge,
shaking him awake. It was 1956
in a suburb in America.

When he saw where he was, he smiled.
I must have had too much, he said, to drink.
His car was perched on the curb.

My mom offered him a glass of milk.
He shook his head, rose,
and padded, gingerly, to his car.
As he drove away, we waved
and he waved back.

Crown Royal

My father didn't drink because
his father and his brothers
drank too much.
My grandfather's weakness—
Crown Royal—cloaked
in a blue velvet pouch,
cost what he made in a day
tuning the cars of Milton
until they hummed.
He loved to sing the Irish songs
whenever he was soused.

But when my dad
snatched the bottle away
from his drunk brother Bobby
after Easter dinner,
Bobby sucker-punched him.

I was 11, ready to kill,
but my dad, an ex-Marine,
held back, gathered my mother,
my siblings and me,
and retreated home as his eye
swelled and colored.

The youngest, Donnie,
turned to booze when Bobby
ran their gas station
into the ground.
Bobby had filched cash from the till
to play his favorite horses.

He drank when they won
and he drank when they lost.
Of course, he lost
much more than he won.

Hungover Sundays

I remember those days we'd straggle out of bed
at mid-day like ragged cats
and gather the pride in the great room.
Draped over worn couches and reclaimed chairs,
licking our wounds while nursing headaches
with bloody Mary's, recounting stories
of collisions with trees, stone walls, and windshields
we survived before seatbelts required
and designated drivers . . .And the times
we'd been jumped—fights we'd gotten into
and pulled each other out of. Nights we'd blacked out
and woke in strange beds and back yards
and the back seat of strangers' cars.
And girls who picked us up or who we picked up—
beautiful crazy sexy ugly girls we wish
we could remember or forget.
We'd roar until our heads began to clear.
We'd laugh until our sides stitched
and we were ready to break out the beer.

Class of '69

Carl keeps an excel spreadsheet
for the class of '69. X's
mark the dead. I'm looking for
an algorithm—the one
that sealed their fate.

Here's what we know:
A pool at UMass claimed Kurt
who, at 20 years of age,
swimming alone,
mistimed a flip turn.
Nancy found a van
no place to fall asleep
on the highway at night.
Skippy should've had
those headaches scanned.
The brain surgeon Ed
couldn't cure his own cancer.
Paula OD'd on downs
And Sue slept with the wrong guy.

We could have used a banshee—
keening to let us know
and knowing intervene . . .

Now we're getting old.
We look to genes whose code
spells our destiny. Meanwhile,
we do the math.

Quabbin Reservoir

Joe Langland, my poetry professor,
invited me to his favorite spot—
the Quabbin Reservoir.
It was spring, green with buds and promise,
birds singing up a storm.

He surprised me when he stripped
and waded into the water.
Is it legal? I asked. He laughed
and waved me in.

When we emerged
into the frigid air,
he said, Let's dry off
like Norwegians.

He stood behind me,
back-to-back and hooked
my arms and lifted me
off the ground.

Now you, he said.
I didn't think to question
my professor. I was 22.
He was pushing 50.

I dressed quickly and left,
wet and confused.
I still wonder,
was it a test?

Sonnet for the Dead

Though they are long gone, we seek their approval still.
I need to get an A, my sister-in-law swears
Because her mother demands it.
In case her parents happen to parachute in
My wife keeps the house immaculate.
Some days my father hovers above
As I hunch inert at my desk. He nudges me
Back to work by merely shaking his head.
Later, he reminds me never pay full price
For the car I'd like to buy. Mornings, I dress
Under my mother's critical eye.
Until you leave your body behind,
The dead have a role to play in your life.
Would you choose to have it otherwise?

The Last Thing He Said

The last thing he said to his mother
before he shot himself—
he felt an overwhelming sense of shame.
Though he had no good reason for saying so,
and then he had to go. His sister spent her life
afraid she'd find him dead and have to call
her mom to let her know. If only
I'd supported him, she said,
instead of fighting;
over what, she's forgotten now.
The injustice in the world
what triggered him most—
he argued until his aunts and uncles
refused to host and his mother
suggested he leave her house.
He found a shack in the woods
and a job trimming trees. He'd cut
his wrists years ago but survived.
This time, he had a gun to end his strife.

It's Not Always Easy

To love this life
in winter when the sky
is monotoned gray
and the wind
burns your face;
unless walking
you happen to encounter
a herd of white-tailed deer
grazing in a copse
beside the Alewife Brook.
Luckily, they ignore
your presence. Meanwhile,
a solitary swan grooms
its feathers impossibly white,
while geese and ducks
fish the half-frozen pond,
happy in the womb
of the wetlands
causing you to forget,
however briefly, everything
wrong with the world.
Well, if the Alewife
can be restored
perhaps there's hope
for us. The grey heron
immobile in the sedge
gives nothing away.

Homeless Shopping Carts

We love our walking-closet shopping carts
though they fall off curbs and make a racket
on the pavement. But when the streets steam heat
they ferry our clothes, coats and boots.
They hide our booze from thieves.
They can be something to lean on
like the family and the friends we once had.

Sammy prefers the wheelchair his doc prescribed
after the hit and run. He hangs his bags like buoys
off the back. Claims the chair doubles his take
when he panhandles in the square.

Now he's depressed that the police
repossessed it when he was peeing
In the alley. We watch the garbage truck
crush it along with Sean's shopping cart.

"What a waste!" we all exclaim.
Luckily, Sean grabbed his stash
before they snatched the cart away.
It's un-American, Sammy says
eyeing my Thunderbird wine.

Sympathy for the Vandals

Plywood comes in handy
when vandals smash the plate glass window
of the Winter Hill Laundromat.

I can see why someone
might lose it when the washer
that swallowed their coin
breaks down mid-cycle
and the dryer is clogged
with a lifetime of lint.

Who hasn't thought of throwing
the first stone when no-one's around?

The owners replace the glass;
but a week later it's broken again.
The spider web of cracks
leads to a fist-size hole.

Next day, the plywood is back
but the laundromat
is closed—for sale sign
where the window once was.

Now, dirty clothes pile up
like the unpaid bills
that can only be ignored so long.
Can you see why someone might begin
to feel like they're the one
who's been hung out to dry?

Missing the Bus

I could see from across the street
she'd just missed her bus. She snapped
her fingers, mouthed Damn!
I nodded because I had just
missed the bus many times—
too many to count. If only
we'd gotten up with the alarm,
left the house sooner,
learned to manage our time.

If only I'd finished college
and gone on to grad school
like I planned, I wouldn't
be wasting my time
waiting for buses
or walking home when the bar closes
as the last bus passes by—
staring at the lucky ones
behind the glass.

In the Dark

The beautiful, blind girl
waits patiently
at the corner for the light
to change. There are no
cars coming, but she
has learned to wait
for the talking walk sign.
She clasps her white walking stick
with which she feels
her way by tapping.
She could be anywhere
on a corner in the dead
of winter beneath
a slate grey sky.
Her body is a dark room
with the door closed.
It can't be easy
to navigate a world
based on sight—
every step an act of faith.

This Rough Beast

Raised on ranches and wrought from slaughterhouses,
Grown on farms and meatpacking plants,
Drilled in oil wells and fracked from rock,
shipped by long-haul truckers,
stocked on supermarket shelves.
From blue lives matter to all lives matter,
from Evangelicals to Catholics to Zionists,
from housewives to Harley's,
from true believers to Q-anon,
the kingdom of real Americans
rises like a sphinx out of the dust of the past,
turning fear into rage to fight again the many wars lost,
from the Civil War, to Vietnam, to Iraq and Afghanistan,
from the Senate to the Supreme Court to the White House,
America, first, last, and always.

In the Provinces

In the summer in Wellfleet
the sun assumes his throne.
Mornings, the kettle ponds shimmer.
Pitch pines admire their reflection
from the banks. We watch
an osprey catch a perch
to feed her chicks before
we immerse ourselves
in the pristine water.

In other towns *far far away*
the virus goes room to room
through nursing homes
separating souls from bodies.
In another county, it invades a prison
emptying hundreds of cells.

The virus needs a drink at a bar after a hard day
working the line at the meatpacking plant.
The virus decides to post an ad in the personals:
Loves to party and hang out with friends!
Loves beach blanket bingo!

Corona does want you to know
that you have the right to do
whatever you want
as long as you're willing to host . . .

Meanwhile, in Wellfleet, we'll keep to ourselves,
wait for the "All Clear!"
before we return
to the world we once knew.

Potter's Field: Covid 2020

Bodies on Hart Island are buried by the inmates of Rikers
normally. This time the job was outsourced
to contractors in hazmat suits. Corpses
zipped in body bags rested in white pine boxes,
names printed on top. The unclaimed victims
of covid-19 stacked in trenches—a potter's field—

like the pauper's grave—*Akeldama*—
a field of blood, purchased in repentance
by priests 2,000 years ago
with the silver paid to Judas
for turning Jesus in.
(Judas hanged himself.)

Now they are long gone.
But the poor remain on Hart Island
stacked atop the bodies of former plagues.

Cats

Maybe the Egyptians were right
we should bow to the cat goddess—
daughter of RE—the Sun God.
Well, aren't all cats cousins—

the cat who purrs on my window sill,
kin to the leopard who lounges
in saffron trees in Africa
and the lioness
lolling at mid-day in the middle

of a dusty dirt track as we watch
perched like birds in a jeep in Botswana.
This big cat is pregnant
and unconcerned with us
or anything else but the sun

warming the litter of cubs
in her white belly.
Like my cat, Isis,
she is the queen of her domain.

Botswana

The majestic matriarch
distinguished by her wrinkled
grey robes, keeps one
wise and wary eye on us
as she saunters past
our mechanical, metal armadillo
where we perch
like turtles on a hippo.

Meanwhile, her toddler, curious,
shuffles our way.
To say Hi!
She heads him off
with her trunk.
She seems to know
we're only there to shoot
photos as she consumes
a tree or two for lunch.

For now, our truce holds
so long as we maintain
our distance. Still,
she stomps her foot;
the rains can't come too soon.

March in New England with Mookie

I dragged my lazy labradoodle Mookie
out for an afternoon waltz.

We tap-danced through the muddles,
bleary-eyed under a great grey sky,
smeared as it was with smudgy clouds.
The smog as thick as peat.

It was *railing* and *snaining*—
the snow and ice as slick and slippery
as soap beneath our paws and feet.

He kept his nose to the ground,
hunting for squirrels and bunnies.
As I searched for new words.
We trudged on together
embracing our foggy fate.

The Great Molasses Disaster

—21 Dead, 150 injured

1919, the year of the Black Sox,
an open-hearth steel and iron tank,
50 feet tall, 90 feet wide,
brimming with 2 million gallons of molasses
shipped from Puerto Rico for industrial alcohol,
burst its rivets like the buttons on a fat man's vest
and the metal walls flew off like kites,
unleashing 26 million pounds of dark, viscous goo.

United States Industrial Alcohol
owned the holding tank. When it groaned
and peeled and leaked onto the street,
they had the leaks plugged with caulk
and painted the steel walls brown
ignoring the workers' warnings
the tank was ready to blow.

A 15-foot swell flooded Commercial Street
in Boston's North End,
crushing houses, collapsing the elevated rail
and plowing cars and trucks
into the harbor while horses, dogs,
men and women were caught neck deep
in the sweet, brown muck.

Metacomet, Son of Massasoit

—I am determined not to live until I have no country.

Christian convert John Alderman,
a praying Wampanoag,
tracked Metacomet, aka King Philip,
into a cypress swamp
where he shot and killed him.
It was the colonists who beheaded him.
Then he was drawn and quartered
for good measure.
Alderman was known
for selling the colonists
the heads of natives—
30 shillings a pop.
His reward for ending the bloody war—
Metacomet's head. His right hand
tossed in as a bonus.
Alderman preserved both
in a bucket of rum,
exhibited for a small fee.
The other body parts
hung like ornaments in trees.
Later, the colonists bought back Metacomet's head
to display on a stake.
"So as not to hallow a traitor's body by burial."

For Your Sins

For your sins you must pay.
For the sin of hope
your penance shall be cynicism.
For the sin of happiness
your penance is despair.
For the sin of love
your penance will be loneliness.

And the heavens shall open,
the deluge come forth.
And you shall fall
to your knees to crawl
on your belly and cry out
in the wilderness.

Because this life
like no other
is the life of debt.
And the debt shall be paid.

Grief

Like ink smeared on paper,
gray clouds tarred the sky.
You were quarantined by grief,

refracted by time. You didn't mind
the heavy rain, the pain
gone underground, underneath

the grief, despair.
The only trace: the grimace
on your face.

For My Father

I wanted to thank my father
for working overtime
and still finding a way
to make my games,
where he'd trail me up and down
the football fields and cheer
from the sidelines of the sweat-stained
basketball courts,
and the relentless oblong tracks.
He'd cheer himself hoarse
as I carried the ball
or made a lay-up
or sprinted to the finish line.

He'd pursued the American dream
from aircraft carrier
to maintaining machines,
from rent to own, from used
to new cars and boats.
He bargained and saved for 50 years.

He taught me thrift and loyalty. Although
he could be too damn cheap and loyal
for his own good—
this sentimental, ex-marine
so devoted to my mother
when she died,
he never recovered.

In the Forest

The chinook was a lullaby
sung by the trees—
the lithe sequoias swaying overhead.

Entranced by their song,
we were suddenly grateful
for this opulence—

a gift from the gods
who'd been hibernating all along
In the rich, dark loam of our subconscious.

Your First Girlfriend

We begin to slip in and out of sleep as we age
until we can't tell which is which;
or worse, we lie awake as night yawns on,
until dawn climbs in the window
and crawls into our bed
while birds bugle First Call.

Yet, this is the moment you slide back
into sleep's warm arms.
You snuggle with sleep—
your first girlfriend.
She hasn't changed at all,
so young and beautiful. This time
it just might work out for you.

Pedestrian

—Lacking excitement, dull

6,700 died last year, my wife says
pushing the useless button
at the crosswalk. We venture
onto Mass. Ave. anyway
when we catch a break
between the cars
only to strand
on the island
halfway across.

Cars, trucks and buses
brush us back at 40 mph.
I draw our dog's leash tight
and wait for the white WALK to flash.

When it does, we take
our life in our hands
and step into the street.

The cars screech
to a stop. Still,
a few turn right on red
careening around the corner before us
while bikes fly silently by.

Because We Were Happy

We didn't realize
so many were sad.
Though sometimes
as we drove past them
on the way to work
we saw them weeping
and for a moment
we felt sad too.

Once, we were swimming,
and it was beautiful,
the water whipped
with white caps.
We didn't notice the people
who were drowning
in the near distance
though we heard their calls for help,
we told ourselves it was the sound
of seagulls as we swam to shore.

We were not in charge.
You can't blame us
for what others did
in our name. They
were the ones
with the ropes and the guns.

Because we were blind
we couldn't see
the pain and suffering
though we sometimes heard
the wails and weeping.

We weren't born blind,
but over the years,
we lost our ability to see.

Asylum

It's as easy as cutting a cord,
to separate the mothers and children—
the ones seeking asylum
from gangs and violence,
so desperate to flee
they'll risk seizure
by the border patrol
and customs agents who need
at least two officials—
one who grabs the kids,
the other the mothers—
pinning their arms from behind,
to pry them apart
like oysters.
The agents must learn to ignore
the crying and screams.
They have a job to do,
commands to obey
that come all the way
from the top.

Really, it's as simple as turning a lock,
as easy as pulling a trigger.

Shackled

We sometimes have to shackle
the women prisoners
when they are giving birth
to keep them from escaping
after they deliver.

If they didn't want to be shackled,
they shouldn't have gotten
locked up. Abuse is no excuse
for breaking the law.
Especially someone
with a record
who can't afford a lawyer
and needs to make a deal.

Nineteen years to life
the deal Nikki got.
She'd shot and killed
the man who'd raped and tortured her.
She had to save her child
she told the judge.

Wanted: A Few Good Men

You can always find a gang of guys
more than willing to patrol the border
to keep the aliens out.

There's plenty of us rough and ready
to man the neighborhood watch,
roaming the streets at dusk
with a gun on our hip.

And if you need a posse,
we'll leave our whiskey on the bar
and mount our steeds
to track the miscreants down
and if need be, hang them from a tree.

We'll string up horse thieves and slaves
who try to run, and negros
suspected of flirting
with our women.

We always assume
the suspects armed and dangerous
and our shootings are always justified.

Basquiat

Basquiat knew faces are masks
the authorities use to identify
enemies of the state—
cartoon figures
drawn to accuse
black males of crimes—
racial profiling by design.

So, Basquiat formed a tribe
with Rammelzee
spreading the word in graffiti
on walls, trains, clothes—
collages of images
meant to provoke
while doses of heroin
numbed the pain of his truth.

Salome

How much would you pay for a dance
if you were a king? Anything you want,
said Herod to Salome who wove
a spell with her veiled almond eyes,
hands that fluttered like butterflies,
hips that hypnotized.

I want the head of John the Baptist
she said when done. Well,
an oath is an oath, Herod sighed.

In Regnault's *Salome,*
a boyish girl, or a girlish boy
doesn't give a fig
for the fate of a saint,
the knife she cradles
will bring her mother
the head on a platter.

Boom Box

Keith Haring's *Boom Box*
with its lopsided ovals—
dials and knobs,
cartoon hieroglyphics
representing the outsized
rectangular boxes
that once sat on shoulders
like big squawking birds
announcing the arrival
of a walking party—
spreading the gospel of new tunes—
a bigger than life personality parade
carrying hip hop to the streets
and in your face. Now
we isolate ourselves
between headphones,
earbuds, EarPods. Alone
in our own musical world.

Warhol's Marilyn

Warhol saw the way Marilyn the brand
eclipsed Norma Jean the girl.
How Marilyn the symbol
multiplied exponentially
like bunnies in the suburbs in spring
until omnipresent as rap music
she was a goddess available to all
who worshipped her,
though she was claimed
by an athlete, a playwright, a president
and the rest of us who longed for
the generous breasts, hips & ass,
the bleached blond hair,
lush lip-sticked lips,
sleepy seductive eyes,
and the perfect white skin.

In the Starry Dynamo

I can't stand my own mind
                    —Ginsberg

He almost lost his mind as he angled down
the endless streets and supermarket aisles,
searching for nirvana in the starry dynamo of night.
But his heart never failed him in his quest
for truth in the Buddhist temples
of angel-headed hipsters and merry pranksters.
And didn't he harbor an eye for detail channeling Whitman
 in whose steps he followed into the vast and fertile fields
of his mind's illustrious eye while cultivating his ear
for the music of poetry that we all hear in our childhood
of imaginary friends whom we banish
on the savage psychotic battlefields of adolescence.
Wasn't his soul as deep as the caverns of the ocean
with its luminary fish, its coral castles, its sharks
and minnows and octopi. Yet he was of two minds
about himself or perhaps his mind
had a mind of its own. Nonetheless,
he often seemed ecstatic as he chanted
mindfully free of all ambition.

The Death of a Child

Most days
the pain remains
hidden

like a black cat
in the basement
of your memory.

But some days
you have to go down,
lure it out
and embrace it.

It's not
going
anywhere.

Millennials

Pruning is an art,
Katherine said, referring
to her garden
of tulips and daffodils,
rhododendron and azalea.
Fostering growth
by cutting back . . .
She knew how to trim and snip,
removing the superfluous
and unwanted,
cutting away the dead
branches and stems
so the plants
would flourish and grow.

As long as you don't
cut too much, I said
thinking of poetry
and Social Security.
Ok, Boomer, she quipped.

Passing Away

Some say "he passed"
as if he went by
a minute ago.
You just missed him.
He was here,
but now he's gone
and I have no idea
where he went.
Like a bird you saw
taking flight
in the corner
of your eye,
or a fast car
on the highway
at dawn, flying
in the other direction
growing smaller
in the rearview mirror.

But "passed" is really short
for "passed away"
which is more like
the final note
of a piano concerto.
Or the last wave
before the tide turns.

A lingering smell of smoke
after a fire.
It is not a statement
but a sigh.

It answers the question
with a question.
It is the after
without the life.
It is not a period,
but an ellipsis . . .

Mr. Cop

On the shelves in the back of room 211
our US History books waited at rest.
After his monotoned roll call
we left our desks and slow-walked
back to retrieve them.
On our way to our seats
we stared out the windows
where we all wanted to be.

Mr. Cop liked to start the year
on page one. We took turns reading aloud
and in between scanned the notes
of predecessors and friends:
Mr. Cop sucks. Kill me now.

We memorized significant dates,
the Presidents, the states, and capitals,
and learned how to be bored
out of our gourds. Each week,
he'd hand out tests
and flee the room. Honor code,

he'd quip, heading to the lounge
for a smoke. We got as far
as the Civil War.

Dead Trees

Dead trees remain standing—
stark reminders
of what once was
a flourishing row
of ash, beech and birch.

Now they are cold statements—
wintry exclamations!!!

They creak, sway and whisper
like old friends
and missing family—
an ellipsis . . .
following the names
of the fixed images
rooted in the garden of your mind.

Luoma

—Finnish for "to give up peacefully"

She was adopted from the orphanage
for unwanted girls in China
and named Katlyn
by our single friend Alice.

In grade school, she was Katie,
fashion forward ballerina
who *tour-jeté*'d away from mom.

Underachiever of the smart-girl set
at the upscale high school,
she tap-danced her way to NYU
where she failed to swallow
enough pills for suicide.

Then she changed her name to Kip,
requested "they/them." Cut
her hair and bound her breasts.
Her special friend was nonbinary.

Hormones are just one step, they say,
before the surgery,
the giving up peacefully
of the unwanted self
to adopt a new identity.

The Burden

1

It's a great weight
to carry the future
on our backs
like mules.

To know what we know
yet continue each day
to wake up and head
uphill to work.

Doing what little we can,
stupidly straining
to undo the past
which is a rope
knotted around our neck.

2

Yes, we're as stupid as mules snorting
in the dusty dawn as we munch our oats
and inhale the sweet smell of alfalfa.
The future means little to us. We have
so much work to do. We pull against
our reins and shake our heavy heads
in a useless vain attempt
to throw off our harness. Then we're off,
one hoof in front of the other,
reveling in the muscles in our haunches,
we settle into a rhythm that plays
percussion in our brains
as we clop happily along
remembering the trail as we go.

Anthropocene

The turkeys like to sleep
in the trees, though
it isn't easy for them
to get to bed.
They crane their waffled necks,
trot a few ungainly steps
and lift their plump bodies
off the earth to fly up
and roost on a branch
for the night, away
from insatiable coyotes
and men. They seek
the safety of trees
like leopards
escaping lions.

Lions can climb up
and eat the leopard,
our safari guide tells us,
but they can't get back down.

We are not the turkeys
in this poem.
We are the lions
and we have climbed
up the tree
and eaten the leopard.

Wind

Doesn't it seem to have a mind of its own?
Or am I just anthropomorphizing
the way we do with dogs,
assuming that longing look
means love when it really means
pet me. Well,
hasn't the wind picked up lately?
Like the rain
Or lack of it, the snow
Or lack of it, the temperature
in Anchorage, wildfires in California?
Still the wind seems mysterious—
the way it sneaks up
from behind—we hear it before we see it
and we see it in its influence
like fear, racing clouds, swaying trees,
sand in our eyes! It nudges us forward
or holds us back
and when we harness it,
transforms into green energy,
turning immense blades—
ancient windmills reconfigured
to slow changes in climate
like a thumb in a dike.

Squall

It was sunny when just ahead,
a toxic cloud bank,
strafed with pink and gray,
swooped in, driven by wind
that brought the cold down
like a hand from above.

Hail pinged the hood and snow
whited out the windshield until
I was driving blind. It was a squall
that appeared out of nowhere.

The wheels spun on the slick surface,
the car skidded sideways
and I found myself off the road.
I jumped out to witness
a tandem-truck jackknife,
blockading the highway
until a half-dozen vehicles,
collided into each other like circus clowns—
victims of seemingly random
complex interconnected fractals.
And we were all together alone
on the highway, waiting to be rescued.

Fishing with an Osprey

Knee deep in the turquoise ocean
of the National Seashore
at White Crest Beach in August
beneath a cerulean sky,
I waited for a wave to ride.
I felt a nip at my shin
and peered down into the murky spray
suddenly frothing around me.
The blues were running!
Get the hell out! My friend called.
They'll eat you alive!
I skipped back to shore
where we watched in wonder
as the water keened with life—
a thousand fish swimming and leaping before us.

Then I caught the shadow of a bird,
wings as wide as I am tall,
darkening the sand at my feet.
I glanced up at the beak
and white belly of an osprey.
He flew straight out from my line of vision,
dove and plucked a beautiful silver-blue fish
right out of the school
and wheeled back in a graceful arc
to perch with his feast
on the edge of the dunes.
For that brief sluice in time,
I felt as if I'd flown and fished with him.

New Year's Eve, Florida

We emerged from our evening cocoon
into the back yard at midnight—
the Wolf Moon gleaming so brightly,
we had to look away. The sky

preternatural blue—it might
have been mid-day
except for the stars,
brilliant between the cumulonimbus drifts.

Our dog pranced happily on the grass
while we held hands and laughed.
as the new year began
fraught with peril and promise.
We waited for the wolf to howl.

Freedom and the Dignity It Contains

With hayseed in my hair, I went to Massachusetts,
the most cultured state in the Union, to take a few lessons
in deportment.

—Lincoln, 1848

His humility seems so foreign
in our narcissistic age-a page
from a book we can no longer read
and yet the seeds of hope he planted
sprout in the spring in our hearts.

We search for the conviction and courage,
he displayed, fighting to preserve,
not only his ideas of freedom,
and the dignity it contains,
but the union of a land
divided still today, blinded
by bigotry and hate. How easy
it is to blame others for our faults.

Like another Abraham,
he was called to recreate a nation.
He stood firm to all assaults
as if already carved in rock.
And though he was finally slain,
his efforts point the way to the path
we need to follow If we're to emerge
from darkness into the light of day.

About the Author

Ed Meek is the author of four books of poetry and a collection of short stories. He has had work in *The Sun, The Paris Review, Plume, The North American Review,* and *The Boston Globe.* He writes book reviews for *The Arts Fuse* and is a contributing editor for *The Rivanna Review.* He teaches creative writing at the Osher Lifelong Learning Institute. He lives in Great Barrington with his wife Elizabeth and their labradoodle Mookie.